AN UN-ALPHABET BOOK

HEIDI'S ZOO

by Heidi Goennel

TAMBOURINE BOOKS

NEW YORK

ABCDEFGHIJKLM

NOPQRSTUVWXYZ

To Peter

Library of Congress Cataloging in Publication Data

Goennel, Heidi. Heidi's Zoo: An Un-alphabet book / by Heidi Goennel. p. cm.
Summary: Each double-page spread combines two letters of the alphabet
with two zoo animals or objects beginning with those letters.
1. English language—Alphabet—Juvenile literature. 2. Zoos—Juvenile
literature.   [1. Alphabet. 2. Zoos. 3. Zoo animals.] I. Title.
PE1155.G64 1993 [E]—dc20 92-16367 CIP AC
ISBN 0-688-12109-8. — ISBN 0-688-12110-1 (lib. bdg.)
1 3 5 7 9 10 8 6 4 2
First edition

ABCDEFGHIJKLM

jumbo/xylophone

NOPQRSTUVWXYZ

ABCDEFGHIJKLM

cat / fish

NOPQRSTUVWXYZ

ABCDEFGHIJKLM

parrot / yak

NOPQRSTUVWXYZ

ABCDEFGHIJKLM

lamb/wolf

NOPQRSTUVWXYZ

ABCDEFGHIJKLM

ant / ice cream

NOPQRSTUVWXYZ

ABCDEFGHIJKLM

beaver/dog

NOPQRSTUVWXYZ

ABCDEFGHIJKLM

umbrella/mime

NOPQRSTUVWXYZ

ABCDEFGHIJKLM

gazelle/sloth

NOPQRSTUVWXYZ

ABCDEFGHIJKLM

venus flytrap/rose

NOPQRSTUVWXYZ

ABCDEFG**HI**JKLM

tortoise/hare

NOPQRSTUVWXYZ

ABCDEFGHIJKLM

quail/egg

NOPQRSTUVWXYZ

ABCDEFGHIJKLM

oyster/pig

NOPQRSTUVWXYZ

ABCDEFGHIJKLM

keeper/nuts

NOPQRSTUVWXYZ

ABCDEFGHIJKLM

zebra / zoo

NOPQRSTUVWXYZ

ABCDEFGHIJKLM

NOPQRSTUVWXYZ